The Small Lights of Her Heart

New Women's Voices Series No. 174

poems by

Nora Hikari

Finishing Line Press
Georgetown, Kentucky

The Small Lights
of Her Heart

ACKNOWLEDGMENTS

Many thanks to the publications that first published some of these poems,
often in older drafts:

The Shade Journal: "Fantasy of the Author as a Small Girl"
All Guts No Glory: "An Oral History of Hope," "Wikipedia Page Found Poem
for Hatsune Miku," "Post-Transition Glow-Up Timeline"
ALOCASIA: "Exposition on Pears as a Transmisogynist"
Palette Poetry: "I Refuse to Write A Poem About Body"
Misery Tourism: "The Autogynephile's Guide to Depiction"
Opia: "Second Date Deadname Swap"
The Journal: "Starlight on the Valdez Shore"
Anomaly: "I call this one "Not Hating Your Own Kind""
Diode: "Coming Out Letter As A Perching Bird," "Store Bought Is Fine"
Sine Theta: "Aromachology of Penetrated Time"
Dust: "Chemistry Notes on Attractive Forces"

Publisher: Leah Huete de Maines
Editor: Christen Kincaid
Cover Art: Hannah Camille
Author Photo: Cassi Segulin
Cover Design: Elizabeth Maines McCleavy

Order online: www.finishinglinepress.com
also available on amazon.com

Author inquiries and mail orders:
Finishing Line Press
PO Box 1626
Georgetown, Kentucky 40324
USA

Table of Contents

Fantasy of the Author as a Small Girl

In a small voice, she says: perhaps, if
the things I want are small enough,
and smooth enough, they will be forgotten
and not taken from me.

Small, like a small house. In this house
there is a small room. Inside the small room
there is a small dollhouse. Inside the dollhouse
is a small girl with no dolls. The girl who is a doll
has never heard of what a doll is. Instead
the small girl in the small dollhouse
has a small collection of small stones.
She keeps the stones in a tin for mints,
and they clatter around like hopes
in the midst of other coins,
each of the stones a name she hopes to keep.

Girl, like the kind of thing a girl tries to be.
Girl twice, even: first, to char the wood,
second, to burn the charcoal. Girl, which builds
up inside of her small chest until it misfortunes
into a spark from the world. Then girl all at once,
as it consumes her from head to toe in heat and mirage.
Girl as a catastrophe, something to befall her.
Girl slowly, as a secret, and then quickly,
a stolen secret, carried away from her to places
she has not begun to imagine.

I

An Oral History of Hope
(After Never Angeline Nørth)

Two monster girls give each other
back rubs in the back of a Toyota Camry.
Two monster girls have never seen
each other or anyone like themselves
and email back and forth pitch-shifted
self portraits of hacksaws.
Two monster girls upload a PDF to
MonstersPlace.com about how to
biohack survival using common toiletries and
uncircumcised hypodermic needles.

Monster girls know rituals; old magic;
blood sigils and mystic text study
and autostigmata; there's a way to get there
if you have a knife and conviction.
Cost of admission: a precious burden.
Most girls offer an organ. A flap of skin.
Tendons plucked from gently unbound wrists.
Every monster girl spends her life accumulating
rituals and spells to bring about the end of time.
This is what all her wishes are, at their core.

"One day we'll be together,"
every single atrocity says to every other.
"One day I'll be real and you can touch
me in meatspace." It's a convergent prayer,
independently developed across time and
space, in the thick throatfolds of every
monmusume. We just want to be born. We're
just tired of waiting to be real.

The prophecy reads: one day,
the sun will explode, or a nuclear apocalypse
will bless the treeline, or mother Poseidon
will consider us too bashful and take us home.
One day, there'll be a set of arms for every girl,
and more hugs than you can steal.
One day, there isn't left-handed or right
handed, there aren't chromosomes to solve for like "X"
or "Y," there aren't even people left,

only monsters, turned loud and uncountable,
unhung from starskies and pulled from the sea.
Every imaginary girl, downloaded,
turned bloodshed real,
every girl who ever wept
while whispering "I want
to burn it all down,
I want to make everything new,"

I Refuse to Write a Poem About Body

Or bodies, plural, meaning corpses,
or warm things pressed together,
or in relation to each other, I refuse
to write about body meaning the specific
ways embraces are acceptable between
parents and children, I refuse to write
a poem about my body, meaning its shape,
which is wrong, but only in the wrong light,
except everybody is always casting
the wrong light on it, I refuse
to write a poem about my body, meaning
corpse, which haunts me every day,
asking me to build it, why haven't I built
her yet, why haven't I pieced together
the collection of blades and pressures
necessary to allow her to take my place,
I refuse to write about the awful sensations
bodies are capable of imposing upon each other,
like *wet,* or *soft,* or *throat throat*
throat, I refuse to say that body is a name
that means *I want something other than this,*
I refuse to write about *callous,* which is
a word for a body struck too many times to feel,
I refuse to strike any body ever again,
to carve my body into the shape of a weapon,
into the name it was given at birth,
I refuse to strike matches against my body,
as they strain for some moment of weakness
to catch me in their hopeful light,
I refuse to match my body against the years
it is owed, which I have still not decided
to pay, which I have decided belong to only myself
and my loves, I refuse to pierce
my body with light, striking myself pink
and bright, meaning *alive,*

I refuse my body, meaning ghost, meaning I deny
him three times before the sun rises, before
the sun itself can strike my body against
itself until it makes the sound *boy*,
until it makes the sound *I'm sorry*,
until it makes the sound *please*,
until it makes the sound *it is all I have
ever wanted.*

The Autogynephile's Guide to Depiction

Step 1: Defy reflection.
Lying is the closest to God
a girl can be, so do it often
and in the shape of a body.
When a mirror asks about your face,
tell her a story about wine and throats.
Figure 1.1: Diagram of a young woman
as an array of blades,
cutting apart sentences at the joints,
pulling away fruit from vine.

Step 2: Practice.
Like all deceptions, depiction
requires discipline and commitment.
Depiction is a mastery of breath.
The best way to practice is briefly
and frequently. When the dog asks
why it is unbearable, say it is summer.
When the waitress asks for your order,
say you are still waiting for a friend.
Expand your mediums. Build an affinity for
charcoal, inkwell, oil pastel, acrylic paint,
asphalt, tire tread, salt mine, birdwing.

Step 3: ????
The art of deception, like all arts,
is built upon several mysteries.
These mysteries come from the place
where gods are born, which is Nowhere,
or sometimes the state medical records office.
A careful cultivation of depiction
requires an equally careful ear
to the voice of the mystery in all places.
Study avidly places like Vogue magazine,
r/transpassing, /tttt/, Ovid's *Metamorphoses*,
and graffiti in gas station restrooms.

Step 4: Profit.
The coffers of gender are sealed
behind the twin pillars of mythology and violence,
two yet-unconquered forms of deception.
Come wielding your fine arts of the body.
Cut through tracts of quivering argonauts
on their own journeys of auto-perception
with your arsenals of Orientalist kinnie memes,
your studious Picrew icons, your [x]phoria
playlists and your sharpened cumrags.
For the woman who lies, what awaits
is, perhaps, the act of living.

Wikipedia Page Found Poem for Hatsune Miku

Girl is an anthropomorph for real-life control.
First girl was chosen via a contest. Girl wore an outfit,
featuring skin like strawberry season.
She collapsed on the snow. The portrayal of it was
derivative and public, according to audiences.

There is a countdown made famous by the rocks:
how they collapsed and struck fatal on the synthesized girl.
No serious injuries were sustained to real women.
They named her "princess machine," riding her magic
into an illustrated sponsorship and a transphobic backlash
that killed her inanimate.

Ask her about her visuals, her art direction,
the sculpture of her back. She is exactly like a parody.
To celebrate the 10th anniversary of her being rooted a soul,
her falsetto voice debuted, selling an average of 40,000 names
a week. Her name is easily
the most recognizable commercial performance.
The flag of the puppet girls was attributed to her.

She was designed to kill herself, or at best
fall in front of an audience. Users can manipulate
her, shadows and hair, face resembling a dancer,
character that rotates on stage as a weapon.
Girl is a game for a user. Girl is not a playable character.

Exposition on Pears, as a Transmisogynist

You, too, could hate pears
if you tried. You too could pick
a hatred—plump, meat-soft,
cloying, overly-earnest—
if you reached high enough.

They're just not the right shape.
Fruit comes in shapes. Fruit comes
in rounds and oblongs
and delicate teardrop ruby cuts.
What shape is a pear? What is "pear-shaped?"
What audacity, named after itself.

A pear is too eager to be cut.
Nothing gives the way a pear does.
Gives and gives and gives and for what?
To be bright and mild and of teeth?
Nothing should want to yield
like that. To be so simple,
not even to be cut, but
like dancing, like back-leading,
the hint of a cut, the intonation
of a request, and the pear
falls apart. What a gimmick.

Where is the tartness? The way
the flesh should cleave sharp and tight?
Nothing but sweet and grain and give.
Cain himself kept
the pear for himself, knowing
nothing about it was harsh,
which is all that God beckons outward.

No, a pear is a failure. A pear
wants something it shouldn't have,
which is for you to love it,
even though it is easy,
because it is soft,
because it asks,
and because it is all
it has ever wanted.

Elegy for [DEADNAME]

You ended, I think, in the way
most things that are real do:
without a chance at redemption,
or a chance to apologize for
any of your dreams.

I could retroactively canonize
your tepid clambering
as a Devonian tetrapod;
wet, clutching the soil, reaching

for the light and air. Like both
yourself and the fish, life
was never going to be anything more
than what it was. It is we, sinners
of mythmaking, that twist your body

into the shape of *aspiration*,
the shape of becoming something else.

So you never really had a shape
of your dreams. Nothing with a name,
like *Rina*, or *Miriam*, or *Katherine*.
More sleep paralysis,
a dream that haunts you,
in the grips of the body,
in the culpability of the flesh.

I wish I could make you speak.
I want to listen to the sound
of your outcry pressed up
against the glass. I want the crash
of your bitterness and denial.
Maybe, then, this fantasy
could be about
saving you.

Second-Date Deadname Swap

So it's trading Magic the Gathering cards.
So it's swapping old drawings
of hard-secret girlsonas.
It's the sending of the buried photos
of your high school self; a library forbidden to everyone
except the woman you're currently
trying to sleep with. It's clear to everyone
that you never expected to make it this far.
All these escape fantasies are about teenagers.

Maybe that's what these rituals are for.
There's nothing sexier than being alive.
I give you my soft parts for your hands;
all of my names, all of my bodies,
all of the people I want to no longer be.
Your tears taste so hot, babe.
You stink like alive and I love it.
Say it. Say it again. Say it with me. Please.
We made it we made it we made it.

Solstice
(after Kaveh Akbar)

Enter the young December dawn.
Stumbling fresh. And bright-eyed.
Into the new. Gasp of sun.

Look at the best of us.
Our defiant tremble.
Our victory. Of light.
The unpromised.

Survival.
Through the cold months.
Together.

O my new dawn.
O my little heartlight.
We were not built.

To slay. Or be slain.
Despite everything.
Forgive them.

For giving you.
Claws. And teeth.
Instead of touch.
And hearth.

Catch your voice.
On my hope.
We will teach ourselves.
A new kind. Of touch.

Our palms are kind.
And blameless.
And perhaps.
Even gentle.

Keep your cheeks wet.
My little song.
And come greet.
The new light.

II

I call this one "Not Hating Your Own Kind"

Mannequin fingers are soft if you can unwind them into realness.
Plastic has a place in my household. What's a plastic flower? Delicate
and immortal all in one. I love a created thing. I love fucked-up things
just a little too much just because they're fucked-up, y'know? I love a
fucked-up looking doll with patchy hair and broad shoulders. I love
an unlovable pear. In the beginning we were asked to name the world.
It's the part of creation we were given. I get to say what a thing is, you
know, as my birthright. I get to draw the lines.

I write my name. I write my own name, over and over, into life.

I call this one "letting me see myself in the mirror." I call this one "an act
of vicious rebellion." It goes like this: I love you. I love you and I'm not
afraid of saying that. I couldn't bury your bones even if I wasn't sobbing
and I thought I could dig. I couldn't. There's something desperate and
unkind about coveting snowflakes as they fall, in all their spindly and
wavering tragedy. All of this could be gone in a second. All of this
could melt in my palms but I'm sorry, I just need to hold it close to my
lashes, let the crystals see my tears. This is what I mean when I say "we
need each other more than we need ourselves."

Before there were names there was the water—water that hadn't been
allowed to name itself. The water is old, and bitter, and wants to make
us like her. The water would like to drown us one by one, it would love
to seep out of our bones, where we buried her, like a child. It would
love to hold us down by our throats and smother us while we thrash
and thrash and apologize to our fathers. Look at me. I'm in the water
with you. I'm right here. Have some of my breath; it's why we kiss.

Store Bought Is Fine

At the Vons check-out line
I literally place a vial of exogenous
nail polish on the conveyor belt
alongside a packet of tattooing needles.

The homegrown woman behind the counter
has already decided that what I have brought
out to her is a kind of sin. We are both lucky
that a confession booth sentinels
by the exit vestibule of the grocer,
next to the candy-lighted claw machine
and the Ozymandian RedBox. *Forgive me Father,*

for I have sinned. I was raised Lutheran,
not Catholic, but I've watched enough
serial television to know the rotary
articulation well enough to pass, as usual.

The pharmacist behind the wooden screen asks me
why I have decided to *purchase* autostigmata.
Confessing to her is easy; lying is the only thing
that takes a passing guide nowadays.
Forgive me Father but I was born unmarked;
I was born with a smooth side and empty hands.

What I mean is that I was actually born
unwounded, regrettably, and I have been
catching up my whole life. I say again
Forgive me, Father,
for I don't know what else to do. I see
all these women with their dimpled palms
and pouring sides and I think about the sin
of coveting that which is my neighbor's.

Perhaps coveting is my intrinsic sin,
in the way that the intrinsic sin of humans
is longing, or the intrinsic sin of matter
is gravity. I say Father forgive me,
I want things I cannot make
in my own home. I covet a natural thing
in the way that a lost balloon covets
the upper firmament. I wish I could tell you
what she says but I have already covered my ears
with weeping. I wish she would say she loves
me, of course, but I also wish she would invite me home.
I wish she would say: *you already have*
everything you need.

I know you are everything
that you say that you are.

Starlight on the Valdez Shore

The stars quiver and fall
one by one, into the crimson skirmish
of the horizon. Imagine a desire held
with both hands, unbloodied, meaning unrealized.
Night blinks amidst the glare
of everything crying out to everything else.
Night trembles in her hands, her fingers
fumbling with the small lights of her heart.
I am holding everything I had ever hoped.
Through my tears I drop each into the water.
Blink. A streak of ruby lipstick on a white dress.
Blink. A champagne flute left forgotten on gold tablecloth.
Blink. Yellow daffodils and white calla lilies.
Hair to the elbows. A toppled cross.
The color violet. An overcast Sunday spent gardening.
Fingers. A smooth throat. The sound of thunder.

Coming Out Letter as a Perching Bird

& I would have sixteen different ways
to tell you what a homebrew girl is,
like throat all over, & "a body is a body
until it isn't," & "the paper birch bursts
from the black earth like a firecracker,
laughing the whole way about the birth of the moon,"

or I could describe it as a contest of wills,
between the grip of God's mangled fist clenched around
my loins & my heart struggling to spread wings
out from my gnashing teeth. I believe in

humanity's ability to fly, & I believe in
incomplete systems, & I believe not everything
that exists can be eaten by logic
or desire. I believe in burning
a preemptive autoeulogy in the same trash bin
as a birth certificate. I don't believe in birth
certificates, or birth names, or birth in the singular.

My lovely yearbook of tendernamed
second girls is called "Once dead,
twice immortal." Nothing about us is dead,
not the futures we left in the care of your dreams,
not the organs we plattered to heaven to feed our becoming,
not even our names, despite what we would say to still you.

I kept a bird locked in my jaws. Fed her saltwater tears
& sour candy. She grew up bright pink & bristling
with indignation. Her feathers were made up of knitted
pronouns that haven't been invented yet. Her hands were
hands & her wings were wings & her dreams
were the shape of high vaulted ceilings,
because she didn't know how to ask for sky. She was gendered

through the hands & the feet & the side & she was called
Isaac. She was called Bound-On-The-Mountain. Her real name was
true & secret. Her real name was a thing yet unseen by anyone.
Her real name was being thrown from my balcony.
Goodbye. Goodbye. Goodbye. You are all so small from here.

On The Length of Names

A chosen name is a kind of gender. By which I mean a chosen name is a kind of thing you already are but also a thing you choose to become because you have decided it is right for you. A name is an important kind of gender because it is the one that you introduce yourself to the world as. I have a very long name. Most people know me as Nora or Hikari or maybe Wires but these are just nicknames and my true name is actually much longer. My name is every single word I will ever write or say in order from my birth until my death. I am never saying anything except my own name. What this means is that words are a kind of identity. Even when you are lying you are showing people what kind of a person you are. When I am saying Good morning! I am a Good Morning kind of person. When I say I don't know if I look good in this dress I am a kind of person who wants to look good in a dress. When I say "I love you" it is a moment in which I have met you and out of the shape of my life the part of my name you get to share in is love. Equally, when I say "I hate you" it is because I am a kind of hate while you are here. I am never finished saying my name because I am never finished becoming. It is silly to be caught up with the habits of drafting and cutting and editing. Your name will never be edited or cut. Once parts of your name are spoken, that is the only time they will ever be spoken, and that moment is indelibly carved onto your body. Or it would be if permanence were real but as all girls who pick a new name all the time know, permanence is also a state in flux. It is a kind of joke, or play. Like how I was once born a boy. But now I was born a girl. And tomorrow something different will be true. When November becomes December I will be a new kind of girl. I am trying very hard to tell you my name in a way that is respectful to every party but sometimes that is difficult, because sometimes you want to lie about what kind of person you are without being detected. This is sometimes called "putting your best foot forward" but also it is sometimes called "artistic license" or sometimes "being stealth." Sometimes this is very important and even very kind to yourself and the people you love. I will do my best to tell you what my name is in the most straightforward way possible for as long as I can. For this part of my name, my name is explaining the shape of my gender. That is what my name is right now. Tomorrow I hope my name will be a kind word to my friends, or a poem about my cat, or a phone call to my sister. Tomorrow my name will still be my name but it will be different just as I will be different tomorrow as well. I will make sure to keep telling you what my name is tomorrow if I see you here again.

Post-Transition Glow-Up Timeline

Little boys on the cusp
of manhood are many things,
like cruel, and salted,
and of star anise.
This boy, fingers dusted
with char and sod, is still wet.

"When I grow up I want to be
an astronaut." Nothing about
airless fire or red sand makes
his heart tremble,
nothing in heaven as anything
more than a quiet luster. Just
a concern with weight,
its impossible absence
become a kind of lust.

Little boys on the cusp of
manhood are told they can be
anything they can imagine. They
are not told they can be things
they cannot imagine, like damp
forever, and soft in the throat,
and an apple buried unbitten.
You can become something you have
never seen before,
something that doesn't ache.

When I grow up I want to be a Trojan Horse
virus. I want to look like a gift
and taste like honeydew. I want to be a small thing,
that arrives and grows to fill space.
I want even the greater gentlenesses,
the ones not allowed me. And I want to be
the color of grapefruit and always at home,
I want to be every kind of boy that a boy
is not. I want to be alive, which means
loved.

III

————

Happy Birthday

I think you could be born young,
doing something you shouldn't be,
bathed in peach light and seeing
everything that could ever happen to you
splayed out like body on canvas.
Tiresias robed in greentext
asking you a question
you know the answer to.

I know a boy who was born at 17,
trembling at Warped Tour, carved open
by the angle of Gerard Way's hips.
I heard he dropped right there,
like an angel, his friends crowding
him and cooing like new mothers,
which, of course, they were,
and he stood up, exactly the same
but put together the right way.

I was born in a crowd, caught
cross-legged by a song about
caskets cracking open for daughters.
I heard her voice break and I cried,
because I too knew how to break,
and so I did. I broke apart like
the bright crust of a melon bun
and went home for the first time.

Happy birthday. Come home.

Anything, Anything

Oh! My rambunctious heart,
caught in the light,
blinking in the new sky!

There! is the bright
arc of the cold,
lashing against
the stroke of sapphire,
the warble and weft
of saffron blooms,
the great crack of
firewood.

I think even here
I would believe
in water
besides rain
and heat besides
blood.

God! I am choked with
something I had hoped to promise
you. I am bitten by a moment
filled to the lips with infant
trust. And would you meet me?

What would you make of me?
What would you ask of me?
What would you need of me?

Anything. Anything. Anything.

Aromachology of Penetrated Time

First, tear through the gurging
membranes of presence. Reject
the wetness of it, the softness,
the impeccable right-nowness of it.
Next, watch as the embers fall
from the sky in that way you always
feared, that way you always
knew was necessary to this part
of your life. Adolescence lashes out
at your ankles, bleeding you
because it cannot help itself,
and because this is all it has ever wanted.

The dust in the nave may yet save you.
Get wrist-deep in everything
that could possibly be a smothering.
Smear your palms with cold absolution,
press them to your face, breathe like you
suddenly know how. Your hands are still
somehow your hands. Despite everything,
it's still you. Carefully, now.
Name everything you smell. Lavender.
Contrition. River water. Grief.
Sand. Soil. The cold face of your pillow,
so, soil. Salt. Salt. Salt.
God, I promise you, one day
we'll forget about everything.

Snake Grammars

Someone I don't know uses the word
"smitten" as the past tense of "smite."

Are we not most in love
when destroyed by a little god?

Utterly brought still by light? Forgive me.
Sometimes I am still my Father's son,

I still measure affection by the old units:
in fingers, in fists, and hand-heights. The red mark

on the collar, a kind of bruise, the fat hilt
of a palm against my throat's sharp peak.

Love is looking up, I think. Apotheosis, eyes
trembling stars, struggling to speak.

I look up and build you into a god, harder than the skies.
Here! Take thunder, take storm, take wind and wave,

all names you might stake for "crash,"
hold them soft to the back of my head, looking brave

as I turn snake, unfasten my jaw, swallow hard and fast.
I like when you call me "tempter." It compliments

my tongue, and her birds. I love gasping in your lap,
as you call me "mouth," as in "to shape unspoken words,"

call me "hole," as in "a brutal emptiness", as in "a fatal gap."
Call me "snake" again, close enough to "woman,"

the first two liars, the two most alive figures in Eden,
the proud inventors of choice and desire.

The past tense of "sin" is "sun."
The past tense of "fall" is "full."

The past tense
of "lightning" is "struck."

Chemistry Notes on Attractive Forces

Once, breath
loved a spark so much
she drew herself inward
until it tore through her.
This is how fire was born,
and her children alight in our blood

to make us hot and alive.
Once, wet loved herself so much
she clung to her body and wept.
This is how fog on the window was born,
why rain is so cold and close,

and how the pondskaters dance.
This is the same way they'll sing about us,
after it's all over;
our old magic bound in the bones
of a world written in things
wanting to be close.

Several Reasons

So long as there are toes
to curl in the steaming nostalgias
of a bath drawn for myself,
and grapes catastrophically green
to forget about and remember,
so long as there are old friends
to miss and new friends to promise,
so long as there are cats who need me
in some kind of infant trust,
so long as there wakes a red sunrise
to quake me from stone habits that
I would name in my grief, perhaps,
perhaps I can live.

Madeleines

If I am to be a dead person I would like
to be also a different kind of thing.
I would like to be a blazing paper birch
or a series of cicadas or a fierce babble
or perhaps a bird or a nice pile of dirt.

If I am to be a dead person I would like
to be all sorts of things I never got to be
in life. I would like to be something
without a past, like half a book,
or a loosened grandfather clock,
or a family recipe completely forgotten.
I would like to be reluctantly dead,
not fiercely, but enough that I didn't
run towards death the way you run towards
a ledge.

I mean if I am to be dead then at least
let me be dead fondly, like a first dead succulent,
or a collection of first fruits, or a first
-born son. If I am to be dead, this time
let me be sad that I am dead. Let me wake up
dead and find myself dead and say "Dead???
Me??? But I had so many madeleines to eat
and sharks to visit and songs to hold
and people to forget and then remember,"
if I am to be dead I would like to be
completely without words and still
not alone. If I am to be dead let me be
as I had always wanted to be:

making peace with my mother, the soil,
and my father, the rain. Leaning up towards
God and kissing her with the tops of my branches.

I Don't Know When She'll Get Here,
But She'll Come Running

Out, from the trappings of childhood,
she unfolds. I watch as she takes
my heart, unwraps the coil of grief
that I wound copper and spring-
tight around it, every day, dutifully,
like a grandfather clock. In pale moments
I would see her; mahogany hair
in a passing window, humble curves,
her whispers in the night,
in deep prayer to meet me.

The woman I would become
takes her medications on time, eats
when she is hungry, weeps when she
can, impishly hoards kind words
for me and my loves. I watch myself
soften into her, my body unfurling
like the river in the spring, breaking
my banks in exultation. Day by day
she would make herself known to me,
like a myth, touching me gently in points
of brilliant attention. I tell rumors
of her coming, prophesying all the love
she might have for everything and everything and
everything. I hear she forgave her mother.
I hear she can cook a mean turkey chili
and will if you ask. I hear she laughs loud
and deep, like a canyon echo who forgot shame.
I hear sometimes she likes to sing.

Notes

"An Oral History of Hope" is after Never Angeline Nørth's hybrid novel *Sea-Witch*.

Wikipedia Page Found Poem for Hatsune Miku draws its text from the Wikipedia page for Hatsune Miku, a Vocaloid voice-bank software and character created by Crypton Future Media.

Solstice is after Kaveh Akbar's poems *Pilgrim Bell* from his second collection of the same name.

With Thanks

Much gratitude to Finishing Line Press for publishing this work, and to Leah Huete de Maines for judging the 2022 New Women's Voices Chapbook Competition. Abiding gratitude and respect to Kit and Pibob for their constant friendship and joy in my life. Deep thanks and love to Hannah Camille for making the cover art for this chapbook, for offering her eyes and heart to this work, and for inspiring several of these poems. Unending love to Maya Deutsch for her constant and unyielding support, warmth, love, passion, guidance, and inspiration. An eternity of poems and songs for Maya and Hannah for being the small lights of my heart.

This chapbook could not exist without the community, care, and craft offered by the following people:

Cammy, Rhiannon, Nico, Lye, Mads, Knight, Emmet, Evie, Claire, Shel, Vin, Reuben, Lynn, Luther Hughes, Sarah Clark, torrin a greathouse, Mag Gabbert, Milena Bee, and noor ibn najam.

My poetry would not have been able to unfold into the shape it has now without the space made for me by other trans writers who inspired me along the way, including:

torrin a greathouse, MIKA/Coyote/Dagger, Never Angeline Nørth, Porpentine Charity Heartscape, Lip Manegio, Keaton St. James, Paige Lewis, Briar Ripley Page, Franny Choi, Danez Smith, Gerard Way, Mia Nie, Carta Monir, Remy Boydell, Frog K/Paris Green, Blake Planty, Ava Hofmann, stupid, Imogen Binnie, merritt k, Isabel Fall, Shel Raphen, Jackie Ess, Pibob, Claire Heinzerling, Vin Tanner, [Sarah] Cavar, Ivy Ruth Langley, and Camellia Berry Grass.

Nora Hikari (she/her) is a disabled Japanese and Chinese transgender poet, producer, and artist based in Philadelphia. She was a 2022 Lambda Literary fellow, and her work is published in *Ploughshares, Gulf Coast, Foglifter, The Journal*, and others. Her chapbook, *GIRL 2.0* (Seven Kitchens Press, 2022) was a Robin Becker Series winner. She was a reader at the 2022 Dodge Poetry Festival and a finalist for the Red Hen Press Benjamin Saltman Award. Her chapbook *Let's Burst Like Stars* is forthcoming from swallow::tale press in 2024. Nora Hikari can be found at her website norahikari.com and on twitter at @system_wires

www.ingramcontent.com/pod-product-compliance
Lightning Source LLC
Chambersburg PA
CBHW022046080426

42734CB00009B/1261